To Paula, my daughter,
for her encouragement

To Loyd, my son,
for sharing his gift of spirituality that inspired
my writing this book's ending poem
"Love in our Lives"

Lunada Press, LLC
Copyright © 2014 Jeanne Maree Iacono
Photograph Copyright © 2014 Jeanne Maree Iacono
Page Layout by Donna Burke

ISBN-10: 0-937176-08-7

ISBN-13: 978-0-937176-08-5

Seasons of Love
Photos and Poems

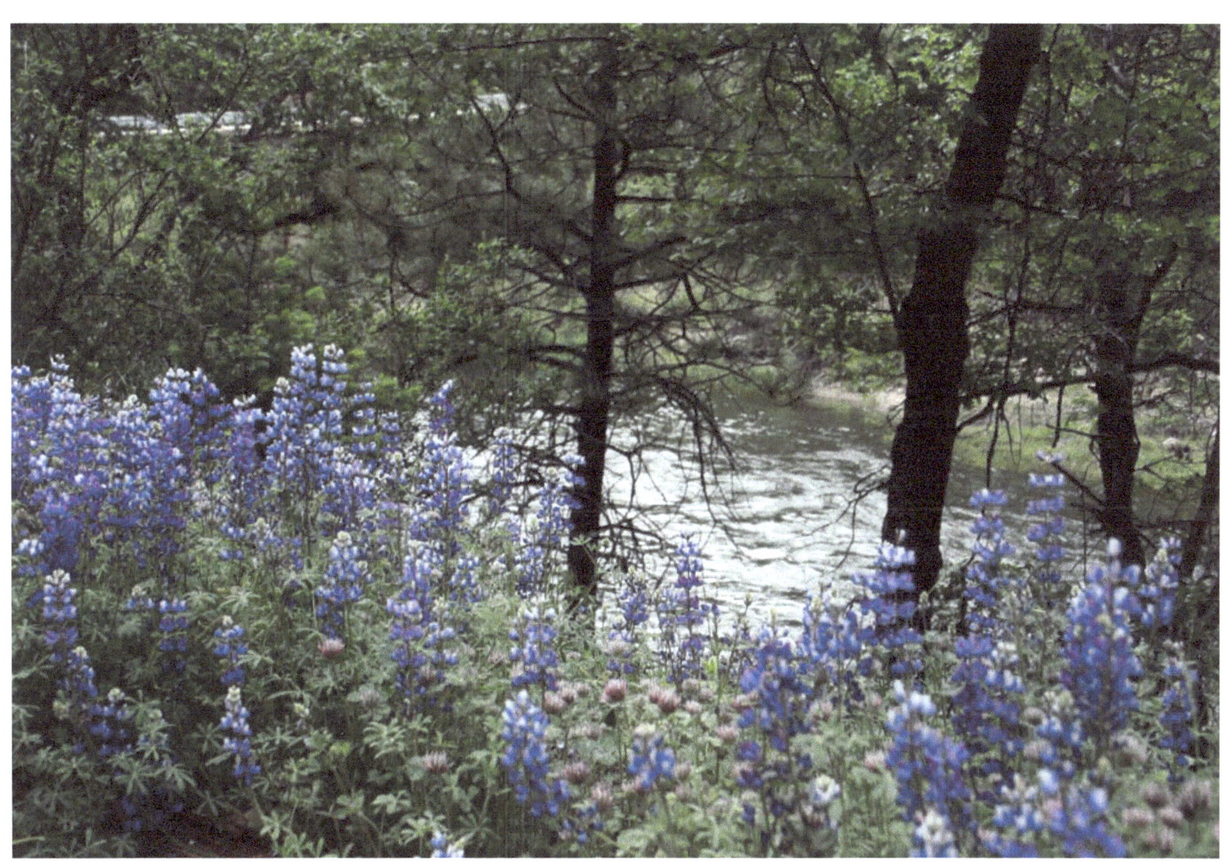

Jeanne Maree Iacono

Fall

Driving up to Quincy

this October morning
driving up the Feather River Canyon
driving up to Quincy
summer season slowing down as
fall flows with the river
then just around a curve
suddenly the trees like courting chameleons
have changed to their most seductive colors
to flirt with fall
reds and oranges, browns and yellows
russets and golds across a canvas of graying sky
blazing colors as the morning canyon cools
light rain, more rain, soft snow showers
and the wind comes asking for a dance
the tempo quickens and fire colors
swirl and twirl dancing with wild spirit
remembering the rite of spring and life's romance
falling colors
all falling in the tumultuous mirth of love
until they flow with the river or lie still
in a multi-colored pattern of beauty
upon the earth
nature is the great chameleon
and her fall casts a magical spell
over all the landscape
this is what i have come for
to fall in love with October morning
this is what i will always come back for
the drive up the Feather River Canyon
to fill my soul
with the changing of the colors
and the beauty of fall in Quincy

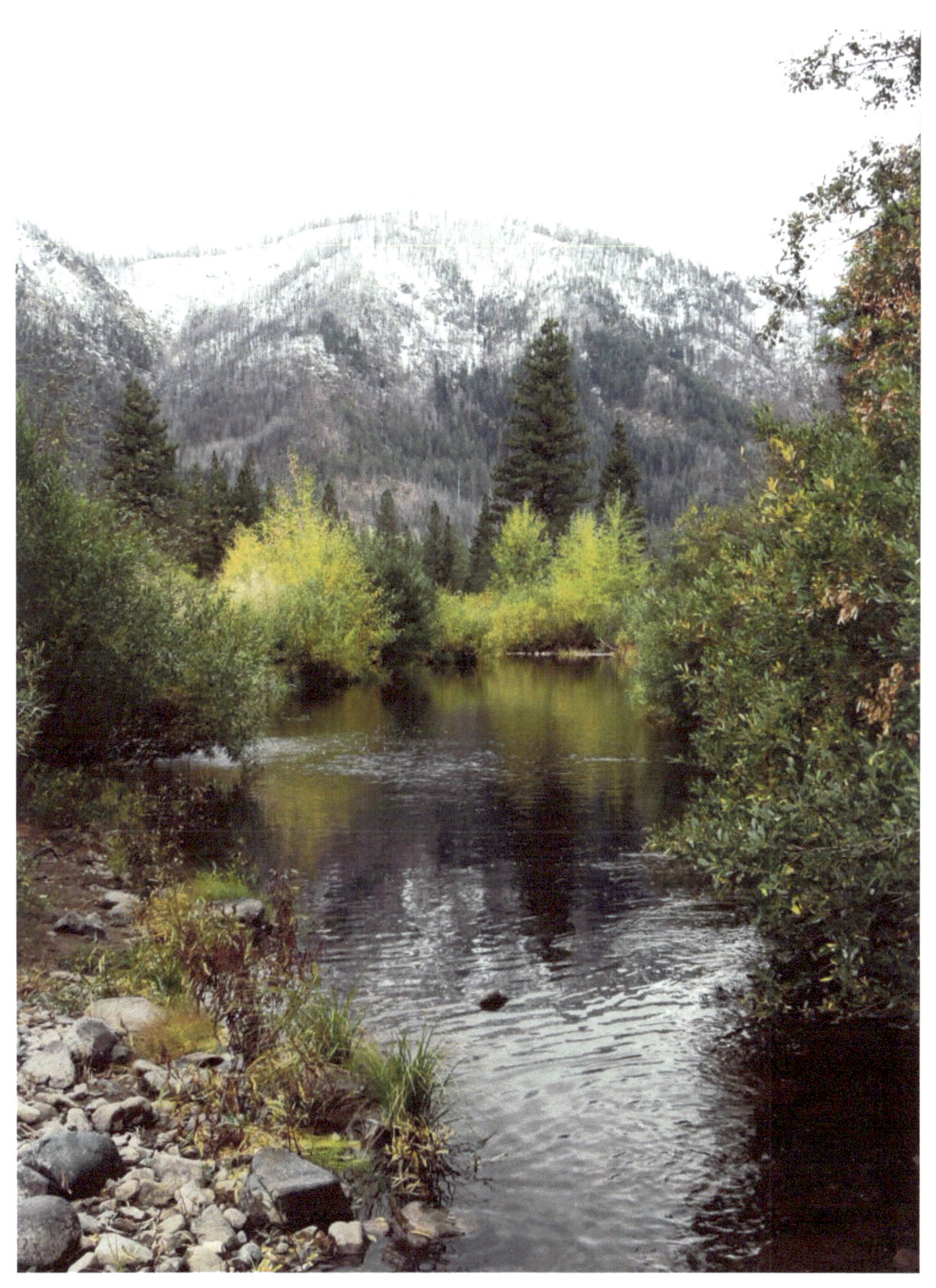

Beauty on Lights Creek

Flag on the Barn

Falling in love
over and over again
just
catching sight
of your wondrous
stars and stripes

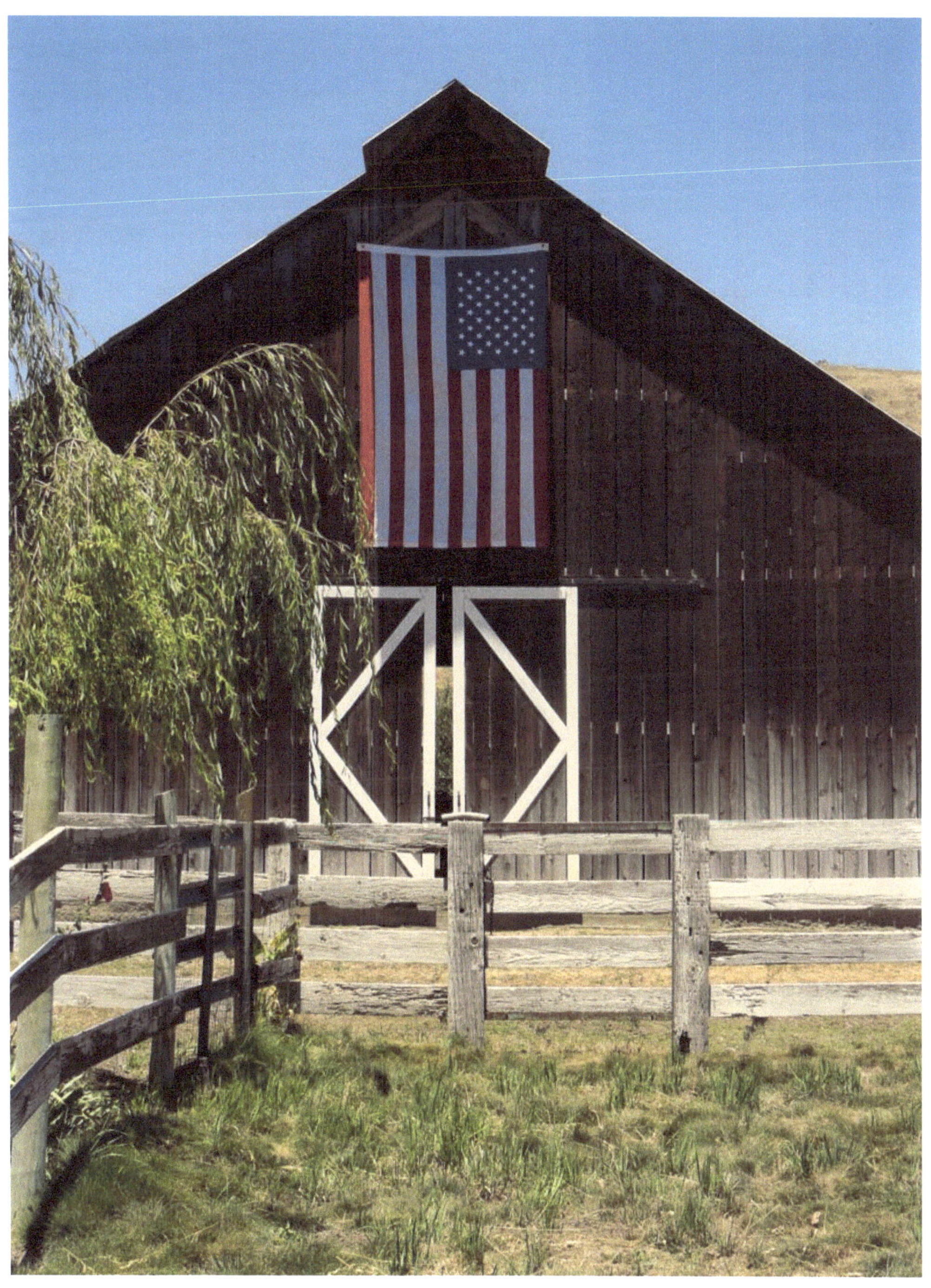

Flag on a Barn

Winter

Not Just Any Isolation

But the kind that arrives
at first with an excitement
in the heart
like the season's first snowstorm
but then steadily grows tiresome
like the falling flakes still falling
in April
until feeling stripped of life
reaching out for just one tender friend
like a branch stretching its naked arm
to relive the touch of one warm spring bird
recalling a few bars of its tune
but not being able to catch the song
takes on a kind of desperate
movement with the wind
before the final numbing
giving-up
that comes over a freezing pond
and dies piece by piece like a dying
moon

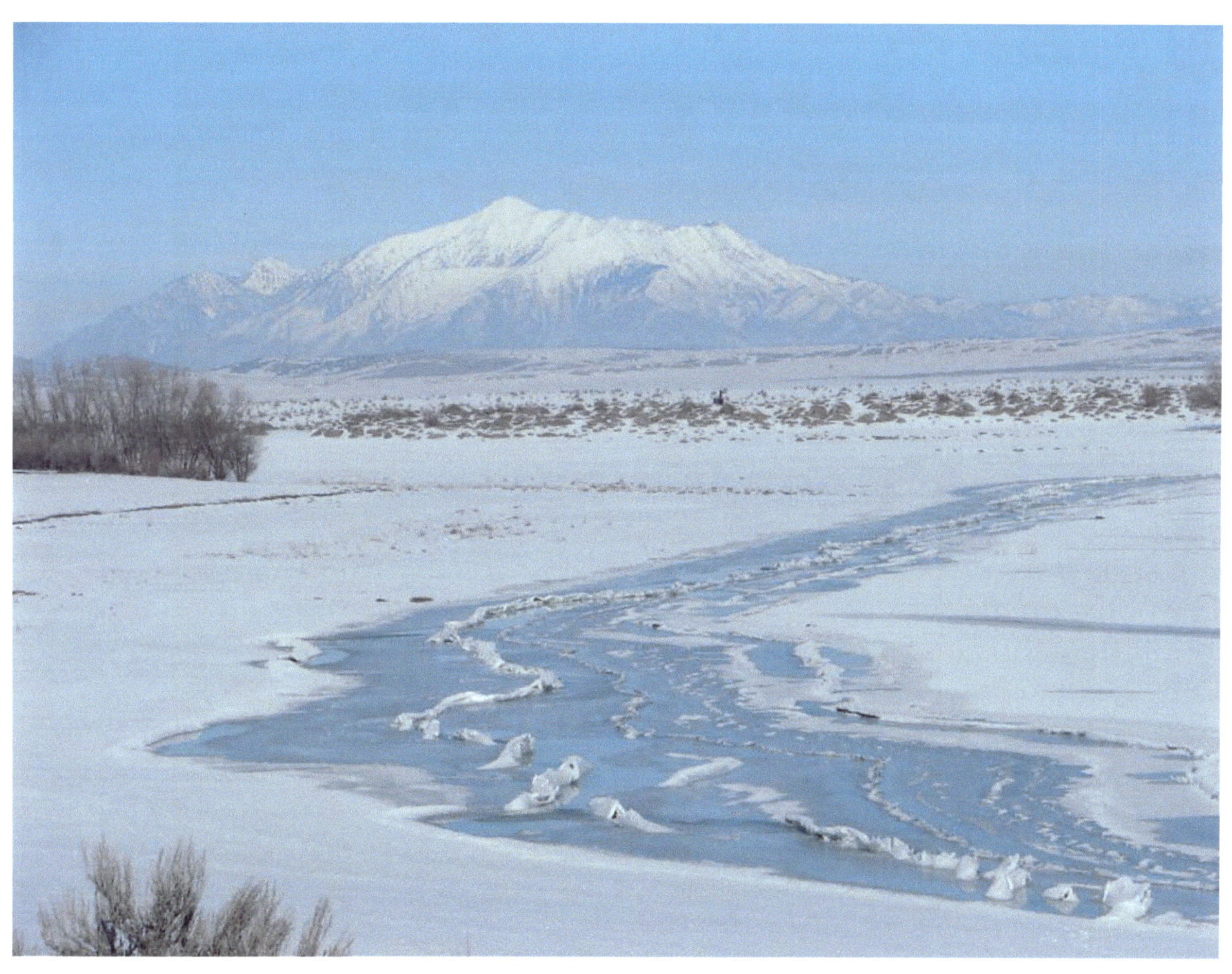

Frozen Yuba Lake

Spring

On these days when

On days
when life feels
as if I exist
amongst empty lost hills

On days
when it seems a mist
lies low between me
and dreams
I dreamed would be

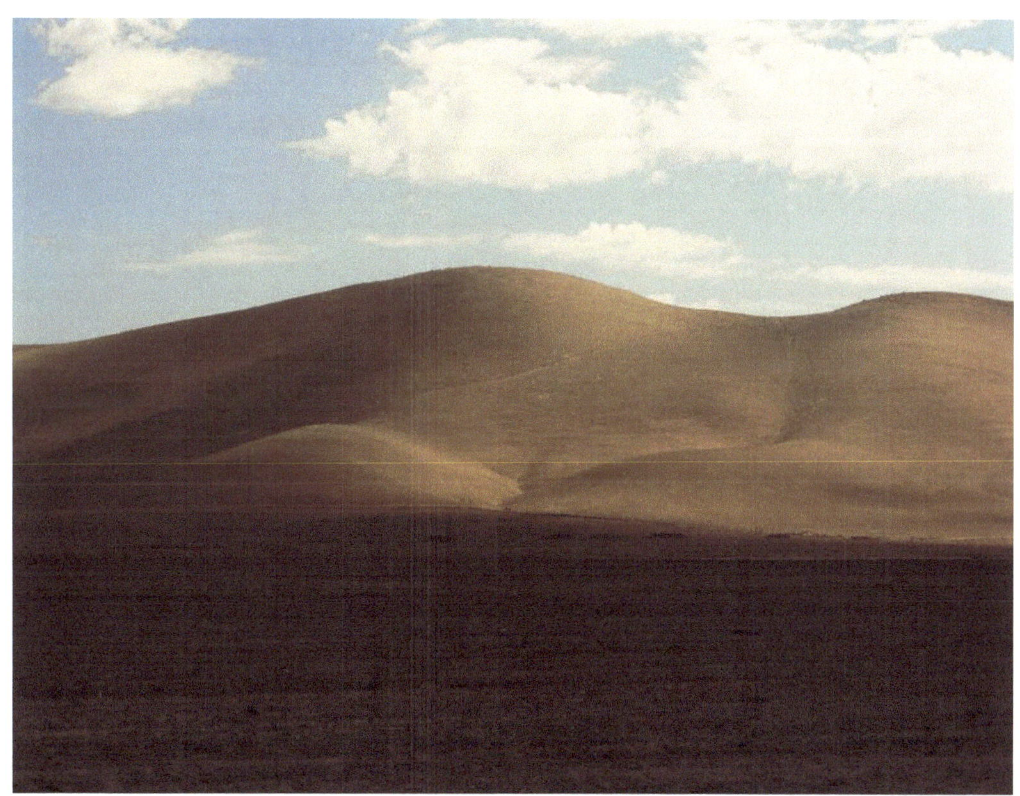

Empty Lost Hills

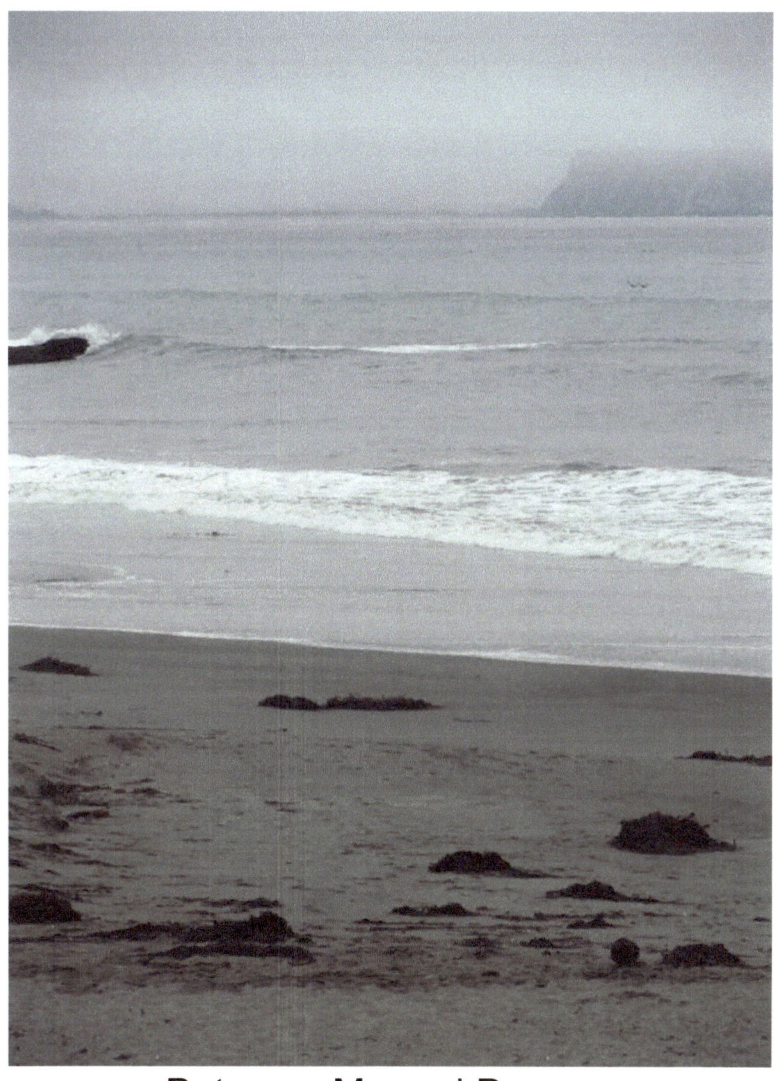

Between Me and Dreams

On these days
I need only take a walk
and faithfully
my soul mate surprises me
showers my spirit with riches

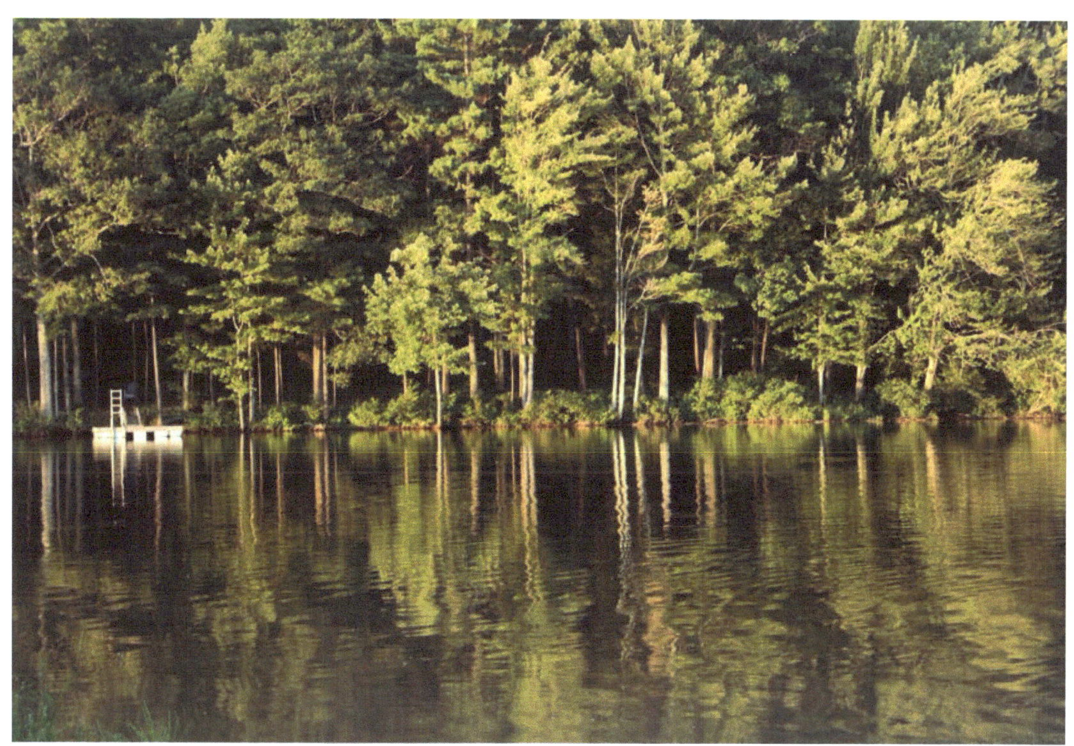

Reflection at Shirttail Beach

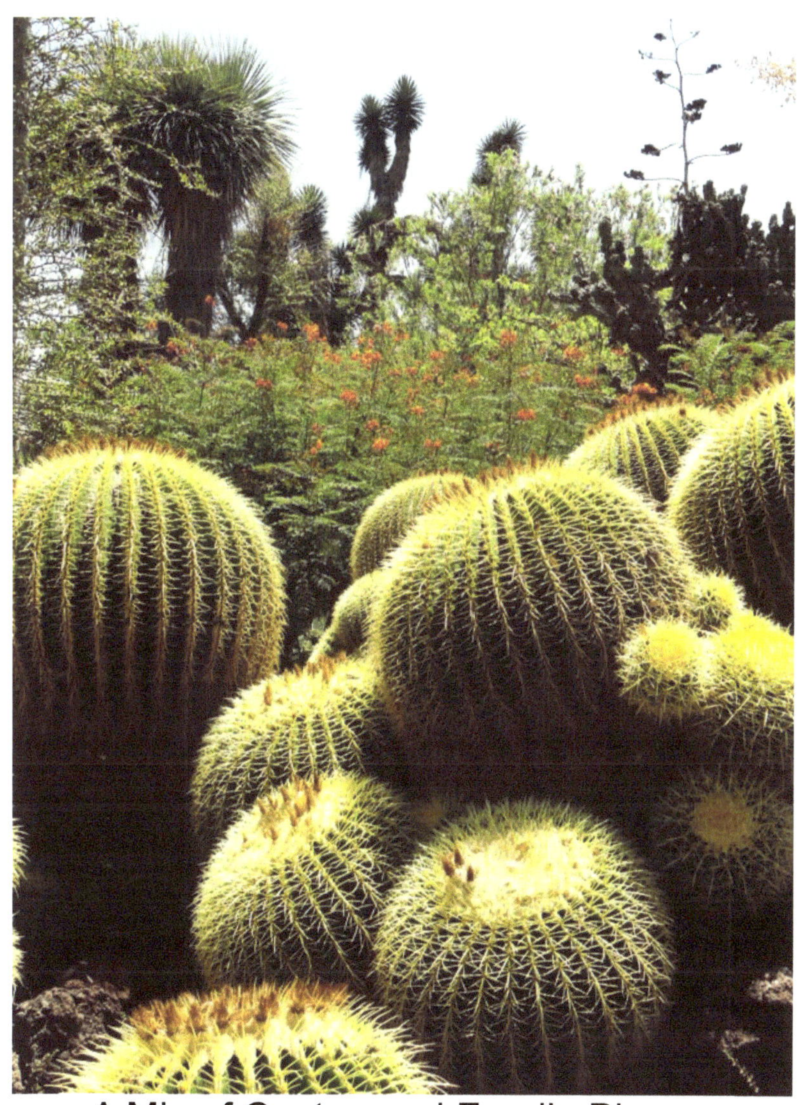

A Mix of Cactus and Fragile Blooms

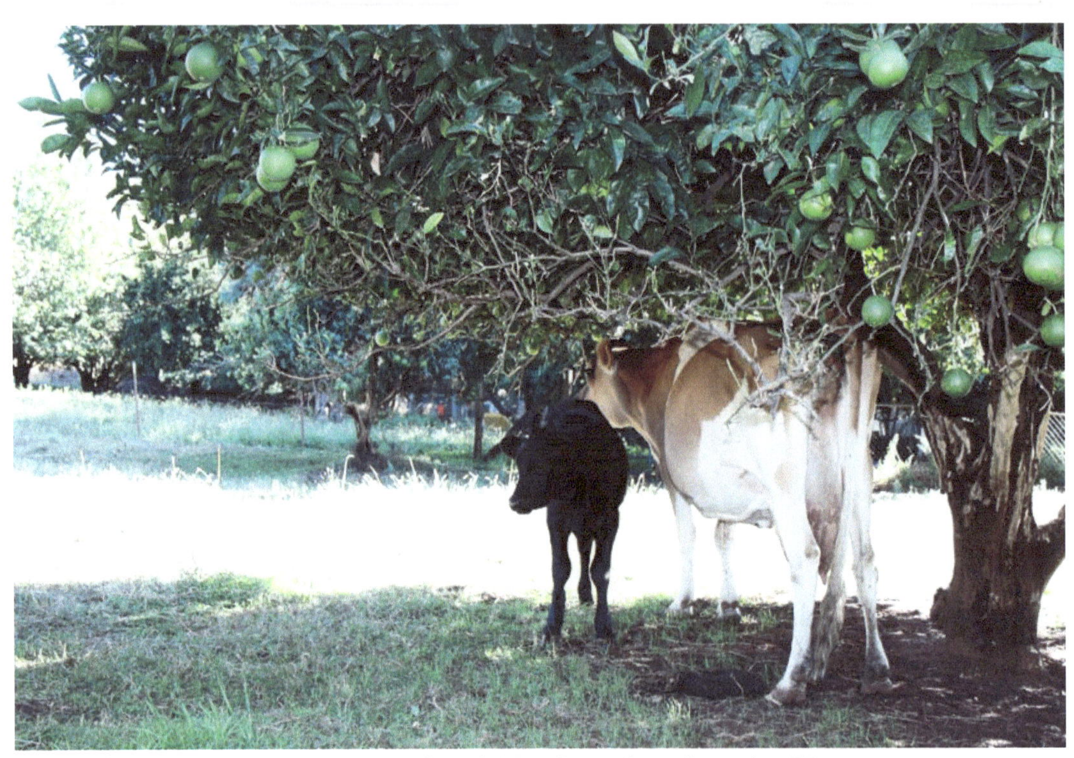

Mother and Calf Under the Apple Tree

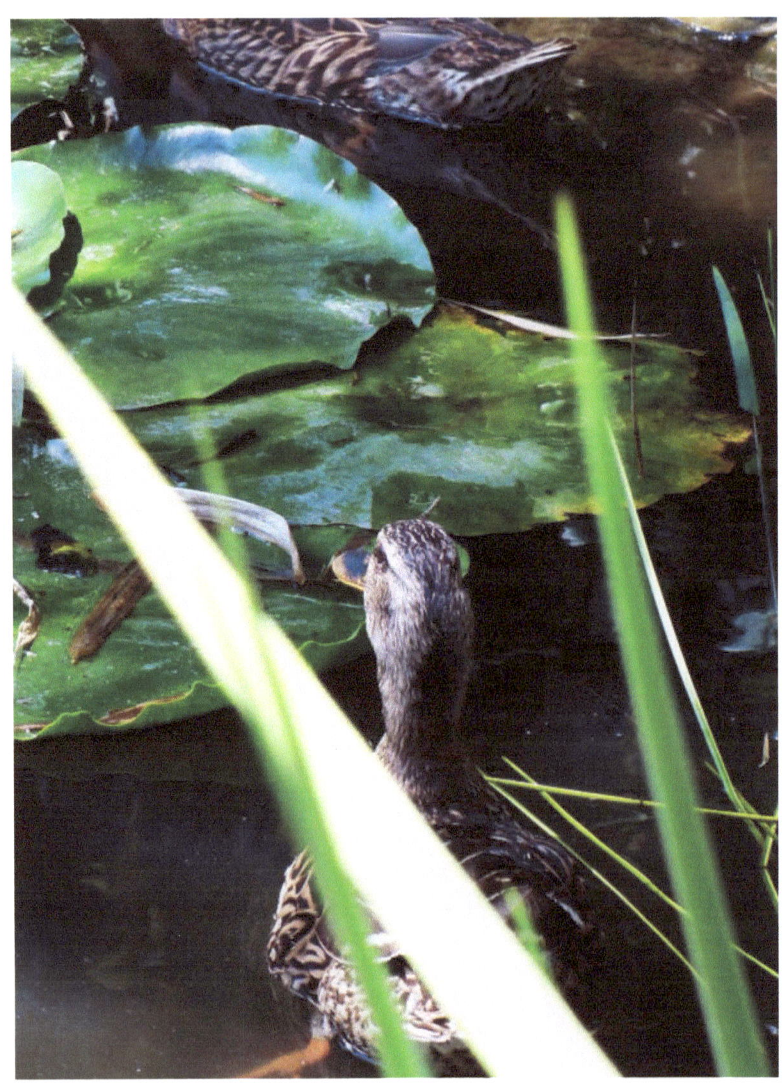

Almost Hidden

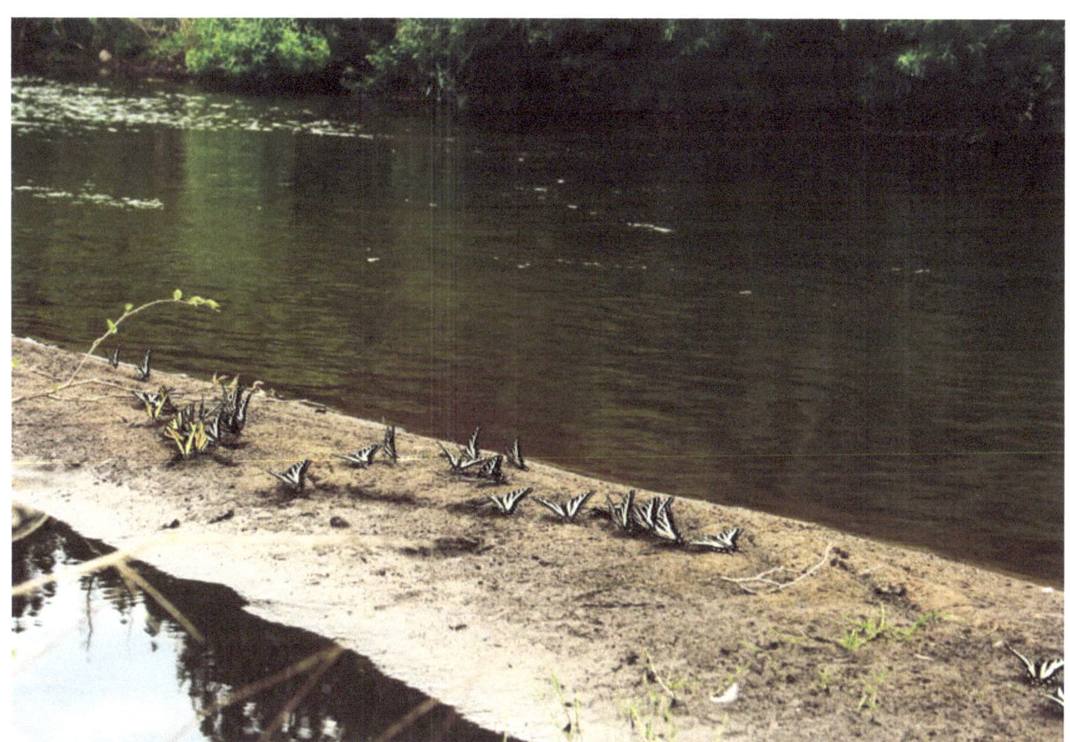

Butterflies on Sand Bar at Lights Creek

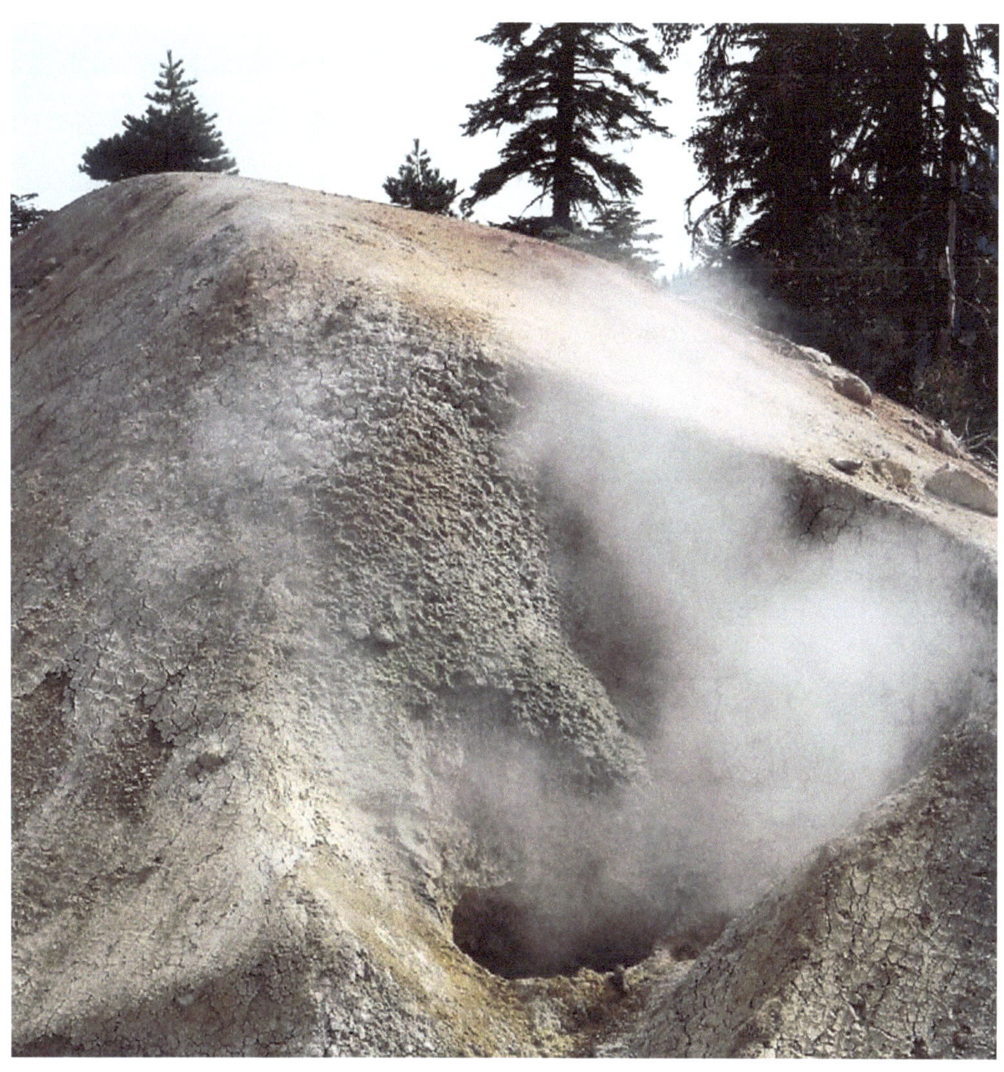

Manifestation of Boiling Rock at Lassen

an array
of never-ending beauty
I fall in love with life again

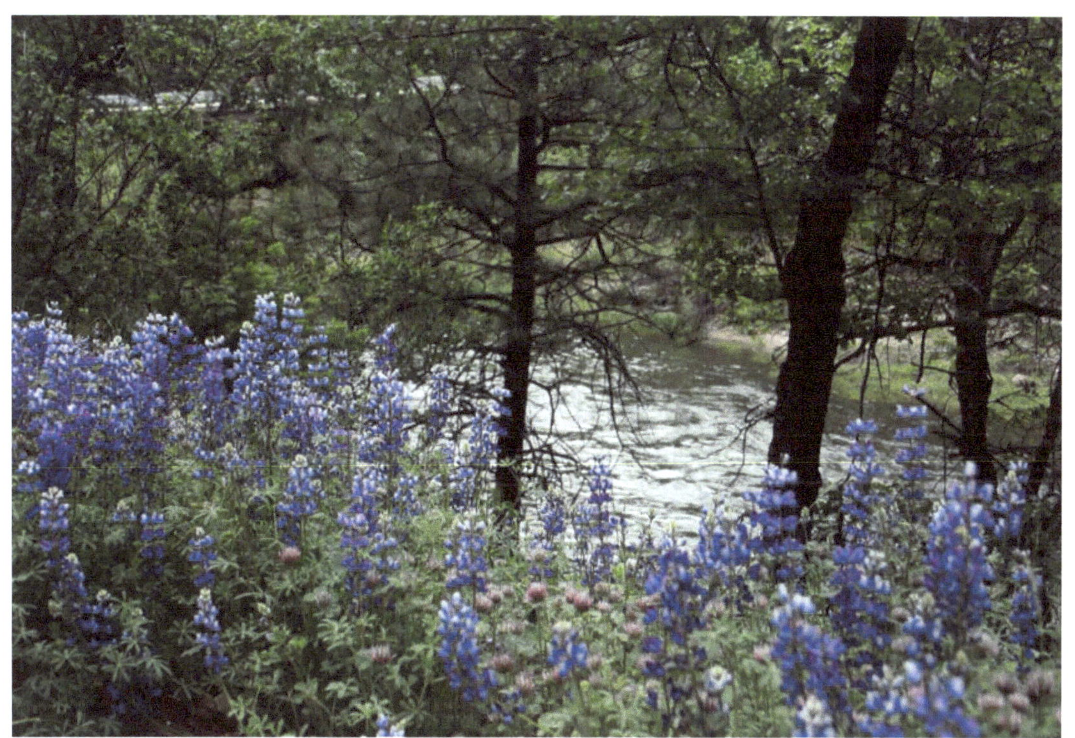

Springtime Near Quincy

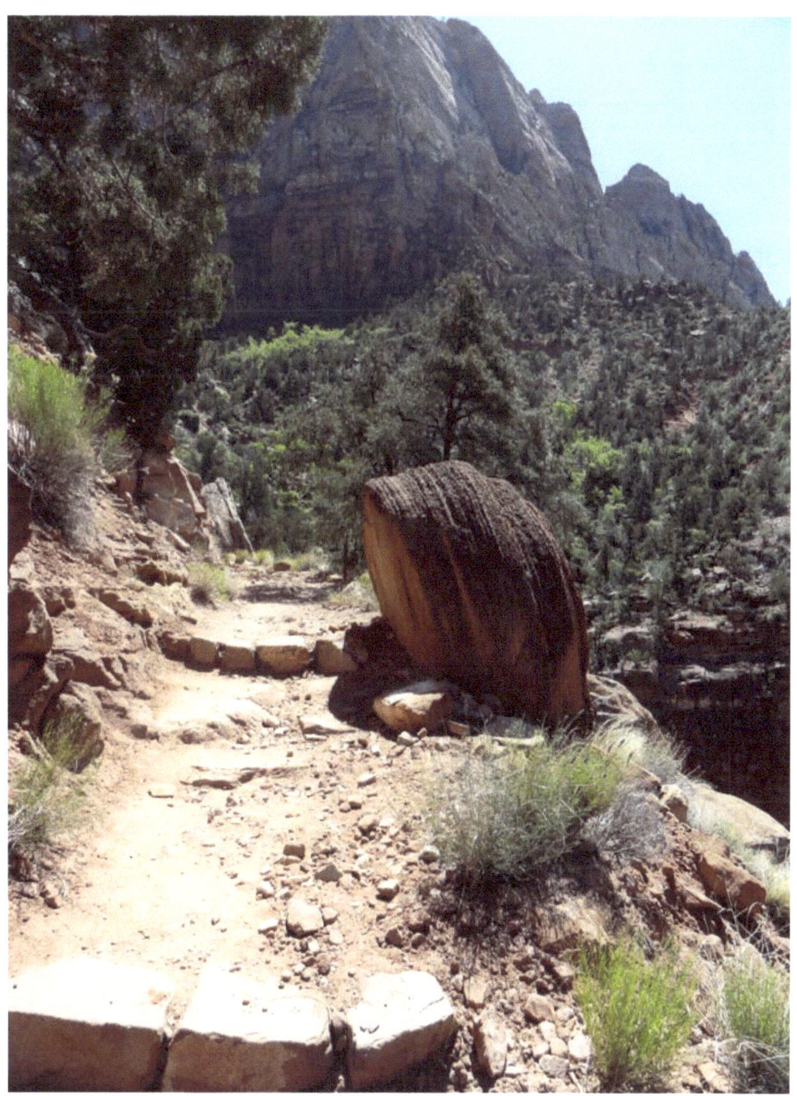

Surprise on the Trail to Zion

Morning in the Garden

mother is watchful
as rose buds open to sun
mother loves each
and every one
she has worked her garden
through days of joy
and days of tears
through the seasons
and through the years
she has tended
every leaf and bloom
as skillfully as a French artist
capturing morning in the garden

as rose buds open to sun
mother leans down
takes in deeply their scent
she listens in the quiet morning
and the garden speaks to her
with the cadence of poetry
she hears the garden's poem
holds it in her heart and soul
until her last deep scent of rose

now as I walk through mother's garden
as new rose buds open to sun
I, too, lean down
take in deeply their scent
and listen in the quiet morning
I hear the garden speak to me
with the cadence of poetry
mother's spirit and soul
has become the poem

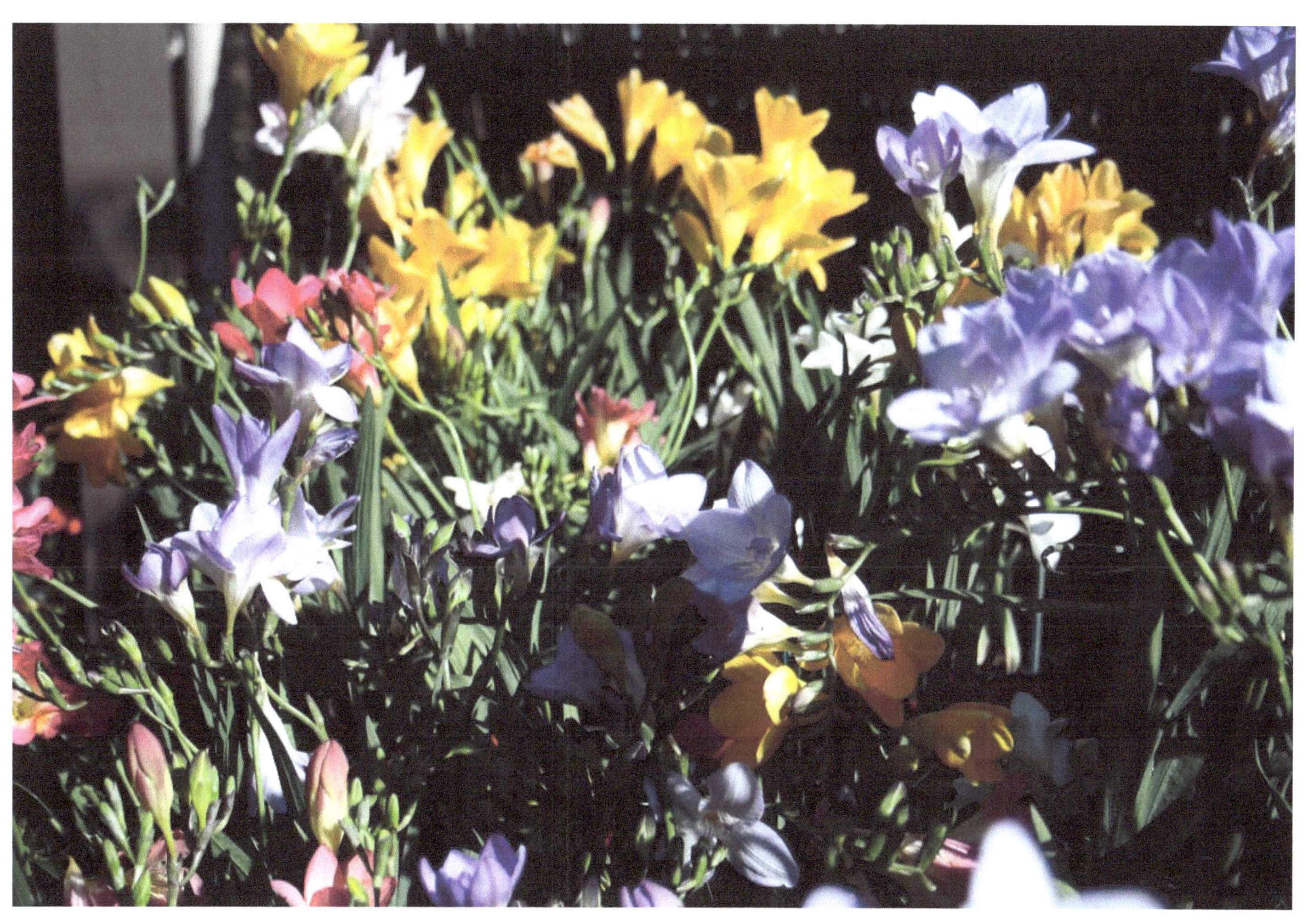

Morning in the Garden

Summer

Haystacks in the Fields

Hay
stacked like obstacles
as a young boy runs
with wonder and joy
through the fields

Hay
stacked with love
as a young man works
with vision and ambition
in the fields

Hay
stacked
row by row
as summers pass and go
Haystacks
sun-drying in day's golden light
until the man
grows too old
to love
the earth

Haystacks
Haystacks
Haystacks left standing
bountiful beauty in the fields

she passes by, snaps a photo
and holds time still
his love not to be forgotten

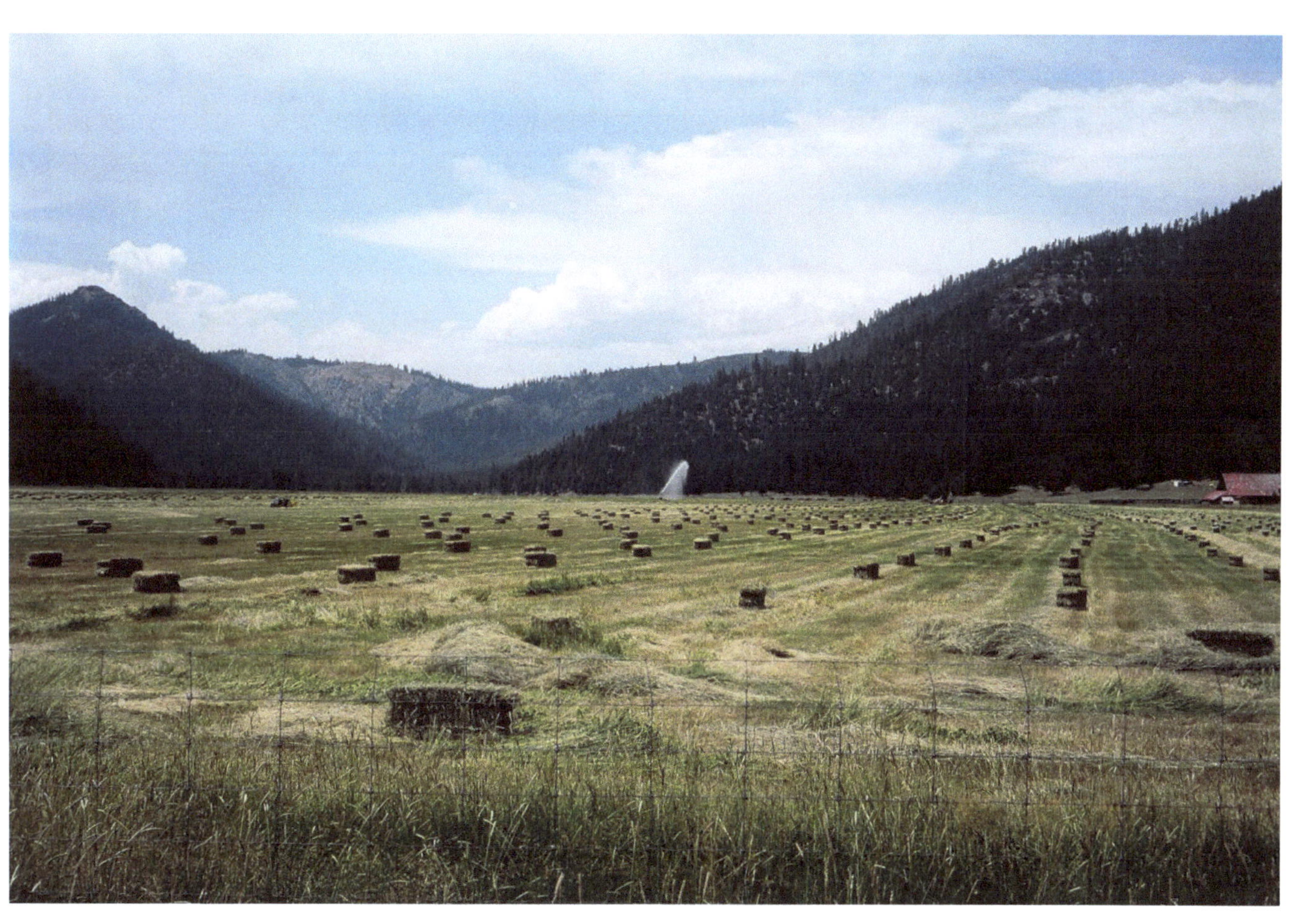

Indian Valley Haystacks

Love in our Lives

that sudden angry burst
that breaks the heart
that unexpected moment
when love is no longer pure
as when arms cradle a newborn
that sudden burst of anger
that breaks the heart
and life becomes the memory of a wreck
abandoned
to the side of some lonely road
left to rust

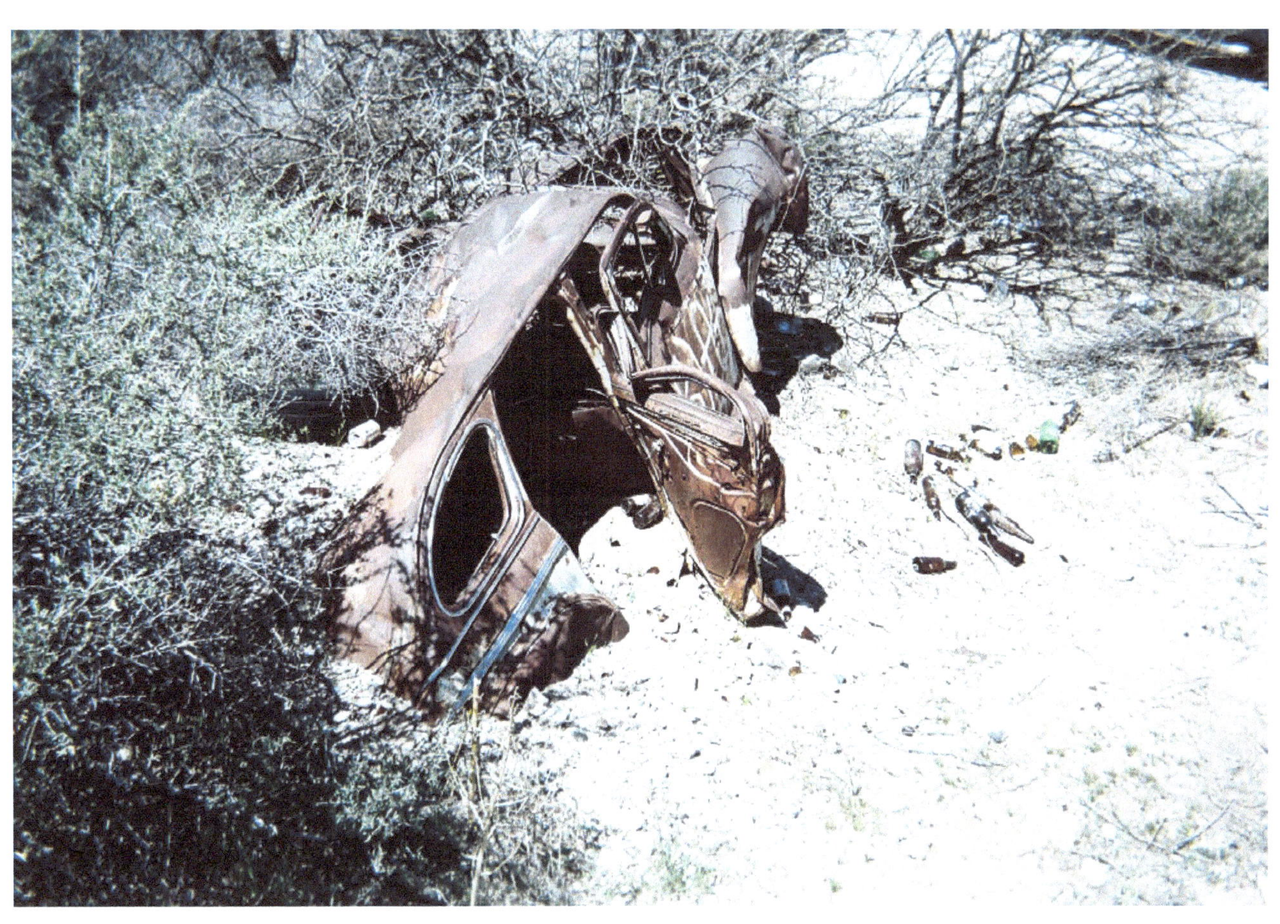

Rusty Car

Only You, God, can be the bridge
over the chasm of anger and daily hurts
Only You, God, can be the bridge
for love to cross
and embrace once again

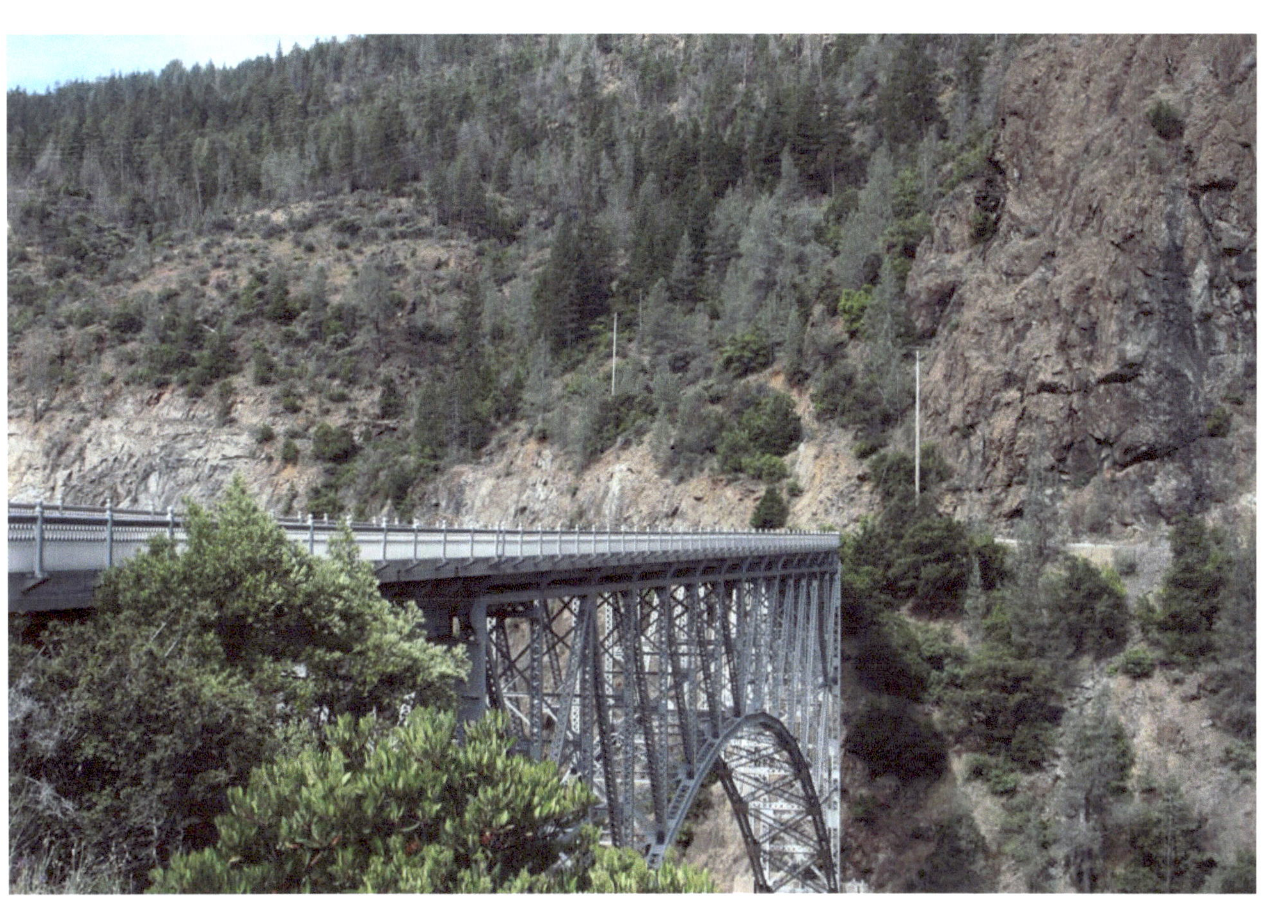

Bridge for Love

Only You, God, can create
that perfect moment
of beauty and peace
that heals our hearts
with Your ever-lasting love

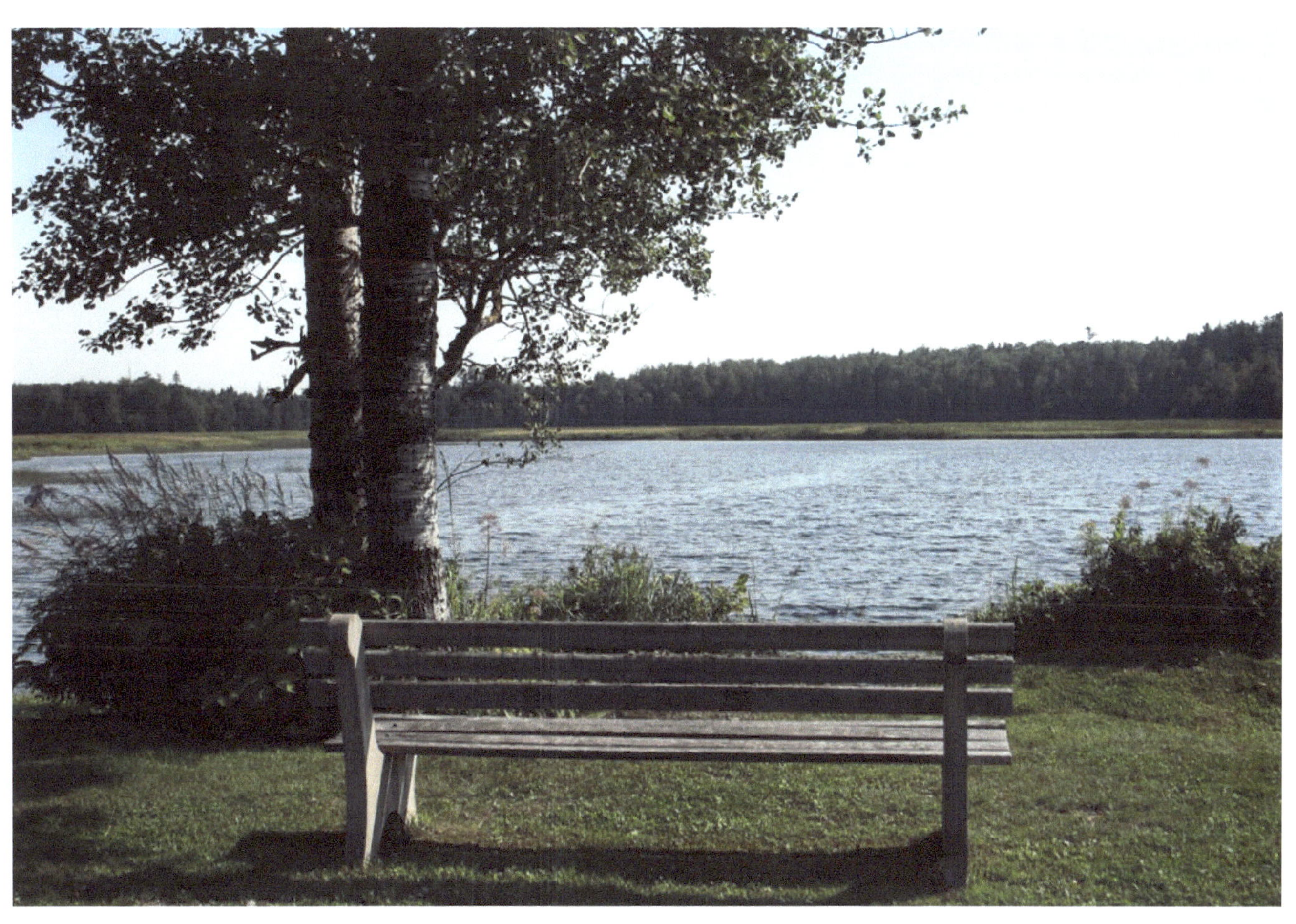

A Peaceful Moment